WORLD IN VIEW

PORTUGAL

Richard Moore

RAINTREE
STECK-VAUGHN
L I B R A R Y
The Steck-Vaughn Company

Library of Congress Cataloging-in-Publication Data

Moore, Richard, 1929–
    Portugal / Richard Moore.
        p.   cm.—(World in view)
    Includes index.
    Summary: Present the geography, history, economy, and culture of Portugal.
    ISBN 0-8114-2451-0
    1. Portugal—Juvenile literature. [1. Portugal.] I. Title.
II. Series.
DP517.M66   1992   91-26998
946.9—dc20   CIP AC

Cover: *Fortified town, Obidos*
Title page: *The church of São Francisco, Oporto*

Consultant: Jane Manaster, University of Texas

Design by Julian Holland Publishing Ltd.

Typeset by Multifacit Graphics, Keyport, NJ
Printed and bound in the United States
by Lake Book, Melrose Park, IL
1 2 3 4 5 6 7 8 9 0 LB 96 95 94 93 92

Photographic credits
Cover: Terry Why/Barnaby's Picture Library; title page: J. Allan Cash; 9 Bruce Coleman Ltd; 10, 11, J. Allan Cash; 12 Robert Harding Picture Library; 15, 16, 17, 19, 20, 21, 25 J. Allan Cash; 29, 33 Michael Short/Robert Harding Picture Library; 34, 37 Mary Evans Picture Library; 39, 40, 43 Popperfoto; 45, 46 J. Allan Cash; 49 Robert Harding Picture Library; 50, 52, 55 J. Allan Cash; 56 J. Reditt/Hutchison Library; 57 Michael Short/Robert Harding Picture Library; 58 Robert Harding Picture Library; 62, 65 J. Allan Cash; 67, 69 Robert Harding Picture Library; 72, 75 J. Allan Cash; 77, 79 Jennifer Johnson; 81 J. Allan Cash; 85 Robert Harding Picture Library; 87 Richard Moore; 88, 89 Michael Short/Robert Harding Picture Library; 91, 93 Jennifer Johnson.

Contents

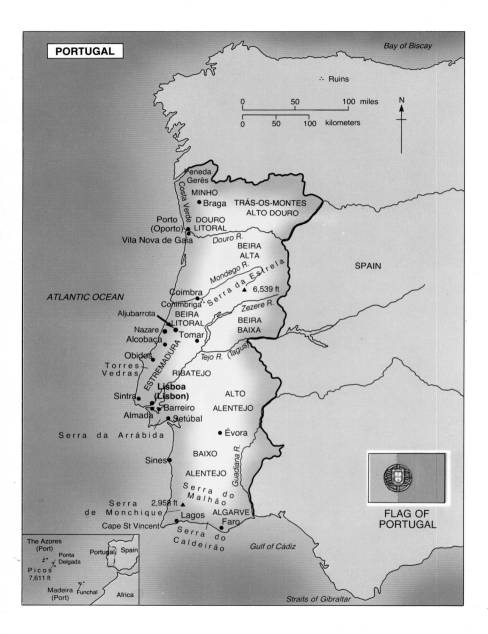

PORTUGAL

Bay of Biscay

∴ Ruins

0   50   100 miles   N

0   50   100   kilometers

Peneda
Gerês
MINHO
Costa Verde
● Braga   TRÁS-OS-MONTES
ALTO DOURO
Porto   DOURO
(Oporto)   LITORAL
Vila Nova de Gaia   Douro R.
BEIRA
ALTA
Mondego R.
Serra da Estrela
ATLANTIC OCEAN   Coimbra   ▲ 6,539 ft
Conimbriga
Aljubarrota   BEIRA   Zezere R.
Nazare   LITORAL   BEIRA
Alcobaça   Tomar   BAIXA
Obidos   Tejo R. (Tagus)
Torres
Vedras   ESTREMADURA   RIBATEJO
Lisboa
Sintra   (Lisbon)   ALTO
Barreiro   ALENTEJO
Almada   Setúbal
Serra da Arrábida   ● Évora
BAIXO
Sines   Guadiana R.
ALENTEJO
Serra do
Malhão
Serra   2,958 ft ▲
de Monchique   Lagos   ALGARVE
Cape St Vincent   Faro
Serra do
Caldeirão   Gulf of Cádiz

SPAIN

FLAG OF
PORTUGAL

The Azores
(Port)
Ponta
Delgada   Portugal Spain
Picos
7,611 ft
Madeira Funchal
(Port)   Africa

Straits of Gibraltar

1 Introducing Portugal

Portugal is a small rectangular country in the southwestern corner of Europe, sandwiched between Spain and the Atlantic Ocean. This area of Europe is known as the Iberian Peninsula and is separated from the rest of the continent by the Pyrenees Mountains. The name "Iberia" refers to the people who lived along the Ebro River in ancient times. Portugal measures 350 miles (560 kilometers) from north to south and 137 miles (220 kilometers) from east to west at its widest point. The border with Spain on the north and east has a total length of 800 miles (1,300 kilometers). The Atlantic coastline on the west and south is 522 miles (840 kilometers).

Mainland Portugal is 34,207 square miles (88,551 square kilometers) in area, a little bigger than Scotland, and slightly smaller than the state of Indiana.

The Portuguese Flag
The Portuguese flag has a band of green and a square of red, with a coat of arms of the Republic centered between them. Behind the shield in the coat of arms is an ancient astronomical globe, with bands of metal showing the paths of heavenly bodies, known as an armilliary sphere. The sphere is a national symbol and appears as a decoration all over Portugal. It commemorates the great discoveries made between 1418 and 1500, when Portuguese ships explored the Atlantic Ocean and Vasco da Gama reached India.

PORTUGAL

PROVINCES AND DISTRICTS OF PORTUGAL

Bay of Biscay

| 0 | 50 | 100 miles |

| 0 | 50 | 100 | kilometers |

N

MINHO

Bragança

Braga

TRÁS-OS-MONTES
ALTO DOURO

Porto
(Oporto)

DOURO
LITORAL

Vila Real

BEIRA ALTA

Viseu

Guarda

Aveiro

Coimbra

ATLANTIC OCEAN

BEIRA
LITORAL

BEIRA
BAIXA

Leiria

Castelo
Branco

RIBATEJO

Santarém

Portalegre

SPAIN

Lisboa
(Lisbon)

ALTO
ALENTEJO

Évora

Setúbal

Viana del
Castelo

Beja

BAIXO
ALENTEJO

ALGARVE

Faro

Gulf of Cádiz

ESTREMADURA

The Azores
(Port)

Portugal

Spain

Madeira
(Port)

Africa

Apart from its territory on the mainland, Portugal also has two groups of islands (archipelagoes) lying in the Atlantic. The group made up of Madeira, Porto Santo, and the Desertas, the Empty Islands, lies 559 miles (900 kilometers) to the southwest off North Africa. The other archipelago, the Azores, consists of nine islands strung out across 500 miles (805 kilometers) of sea, with the nearest island 900 miles (1,500 kilometers) due west of Portugal, and the farthest one 1,200 miles (2,000 kilometers) away.

Portugal's remote position and the fact that it is hemmed in by Spain, with whom it has not always been friendly, has isolated it from events in the rest of Europe. As a result, the Portuguese looked to the sea, and over the centuries became successful traders and explorers. In 1986 Portugal joined the European Economic Community (the EC), and became fully integrated into the European organization for the first time.

Population

Portugal, including Madeira and the Azores islands, has a population of 10,229,000, just over 10 million, which is slightly less than the state of Ohio. The Portuguese people are not evenly spread over the country. They have always preferred to live near the coast if they can. About one third of them live in or around the three principal cities of Lisbon, Oporto, and Setúbal. The density of population varies from 261 per square mile in Lisbon to only 7 per square mile scattered over the remoter parts of rural Alentejo.

Portuguese Money
The unit of currency in Portugal is the *escudo*. Although *escudo* is an ancient name for coins of the Iberian Peninsula, it has been the currency in Portugal only since 1911. It is a decimal currency, with each *escudo* divided into 100 *centavos*. Usually, the *escudo* sign (resembling an American dollar sign) is not placed before the *escudo* figure, but between the *escudo* and the *centavo* figures, 32$50. The national bank issues coins for 50 *centavos*, and for 1,2$50, 5, 10, and 25 *escudos*. There are notes for 20, 50, 100, 500, 1,000, and 5,000 *escudos*. The 5,000 note is called a *conto*.

What Can You Buy?
An ice cream from a street vendor costs about 60 escudos, a hamburger about 150 escudos, and a can of soda around 90 escudos.

Physical geography

Mountains slashed with valleys cover most of Portugal's northern region. The highlands run down the eastern border with Spain and across the extreme southern coast. By and large, the center two thirds of the country slopes down from the Spanish border in the east to the Atlantic in the west. The region south of the Tagus River is a large plain.

Portugal has a network of rivers, with more in the north, where the rainfall is heaviest, than in the south. Some rise in Spain and flow across Portugal to empty into the Atlantic. The three main rivers are: the Tagus (Tejo), with 171 miles (275 kilometers) of its length inside Portugal, and

A herd of chamois in the northern mountains. These goatlike little antelopes are highly prized for their skin, which, when tanned, provides the leather called ''shammy,'' a version of their name.

the capital, Lisbon, standing on its estuary; the Douro, 200 miles (322 kilometers) long, with the second most important city, Oporto, close to its mouth; and the Guadiana, which is 161 miles (260 kilometers) long. The Mondego at 137 miles (220 kilometers) is the longest of the rivers that rise inside Portugal's boundaries.

The scenery of the coastline is very varied. In the northern third of its length there are long stretches of sandy beach, inland lagoons separated from the sea by sandbars, and bays that make ideal fishing harbors. The southern two thirds are a mixture of cliffs and beaches, with some quite dramatic headlands, especially where the coast takes a right-angled turn eastward at Cape St. Vincent.

Climate
Portugal's mild climate is affected by the ocean on two of its sides. The climate varies widely among

9

Cork being harvested near Evora, whose cork oak groves are among the best in Portugal. Cylinders of bark are stripped from the trees. In this photo the already-stripped rolls, looking like long logs, are lying at the foot of the tree. The bark is allowed to grow back again for nine years before the next harvest.

the different parts of the country, even though the distances are not great. The mountainous north differs markedly from the low-lying south, and the coastal regions from the inland areas. In the north, especially the northwest, winter is the time for rain, and the mountains are usually covered with snow. Farther south, winters are fairly mild, and summers hot and dry. Inland, the summer heat can reach 104°F (40°C), though sea breezes keep the coastal regions much cooler. Winter days can be mild and sunny, though the nights get cold. The Algarve, in the extreme south, has almost no rain at all during the summer months.

Animals and plants

There are many sparsely populated areas of Portugal where wild animals are able to live more or less undisturbed. Roe deer, chamois, and foxes can be found in the northern mountains, especially in the remote Peneda-Gerês National Park. The park is also home to species almost extinct elsewhere in Europe, including wolves (although they are increasingly rare), wild horses, and golden eagles. Wild boars here, and in other parts of the country, provide a delicious source of meat and are favorite game with hunters.

In the center of Portugal, in Ribatejo, horse breeding has been an important part of the economy for centuries. There are many ranches, including the national stud farm, where thoroughbred horses are reared. Herds of black bulls also roam these grassy plains, some of them destined to appear in the bull ring.

Cattle graze the lush northeast meadows. Herds of both sheep and goats can be found wherever the pastureland is less fertile, and goats

Umbrella pines in the Serra da Estrela mountains. Several varieties of pines grow all over the country, often cultivated because the wood is a valuable export. The kernels of the umbrella pine cones can be eaten.

One of the most beautiful sights in Portugal is the cascade of almond blossoms in the Algarve in January and February. There is a legend that a Moorish king's Scandinavian wife longed for the snows of her homeland, so he covered his kingdom with groves of almond trees whose blossoms would remind her of snowdrifts.

browse on the meager vegetation of mountain slopes.

About 43 percent of the country is forested, with pines, other evergreens, oaks, and eucalyptus being the most important trees. There are three species of oaks that thrive in Portugal: the evergreen oak, the Lusitanian oak named after the old name of Portugal, Lusitania, and the cork oak. Harvesting the bark of the cork oak is an important, ancient industry. Various species of pines grow over most of the country, sometimes cultivated in plantations for their timber. The largest continuous pine forest in Europe stretches across central Portugal. Pungently scented eucalyptus trees, too, can be seen in most parts, sometimes growing as tall as 250 feet (76 meters).

In the wetter northwest, gorse and heather grow easily, while bushy herbs, such as rosemary, thyme, and lavender perfume the warm air on the mountainsides in the east and south. The center and south of the country is ideal for such semi-tropical flowering plants as yellow mimosa, camellia, and oleander. This is the region, too, for fruit trees, especially oranges, lemons, and figs. The Algarve is famous for its almond trees, whose spectacular pale-pink blossoms cloak the hillsides in early spring.

2 The Provinces of Portugal

Portugal is divided into 11 provinces. Minho and Trás-os-Montes form Portugal's northern edge and contain some of its wildest and most beautiful scenery. The most southerly provinces are the islands in the Madeira archipelago.

Minho and Trás-os-Montes

The coast of the Minho, the wettest part of Portugal, is called the Costa Verde, the Green Coast, because of its luxurious vegetation. Minho has excellent farming land, although the farms are small and often carved out of the hillsides. A chain of dams and lakes runs through the eastern part of the province, formed from valleys that have been flooded for hydroelectric projects. They are surrounded by heavily wooded, rocky mountains.

Trás-os-Montes, "Behind the Mountains," is remote from the rest of the country, underdeveloped, with plenty of hunting but very little industry. This is the area that is benefiting most from financial help from the European Community. Vineyards along the slopes of the river valley in the south of the province grow grapes for making port wine.

The Douro

The Douro River flows down the northeast border with Spain and then turns west to empty into the Atlantic. Nine miles inland from the

The Dom Luis I Bridge, Oporto, over the Douro River was completed in 1886. It carries traffic on two levels to join both the upper and lower parts of the city with Vila Nova da Gaia on the opposite bank. The great oblong of the Bishop's Palace can be seen above the right-hand end of the bridge, with the towers of the cathedral behind it.

mouth of the Douro is Oporto, Portugal's second biggest city. The name means "The Port." In Roman times there were two towns here, on opposite sides of the river, Portus on the northern and Cale on the southern bank. The region in which they stood took its name, Portucale, from a combination of the two. When the invading Moors from North Africa were driven out, in the middle of the thirteenth century, this province gave a version of its name to the whole country, Portugal. After Lisbon, Oporto is Portugal's most important city. It is busy and prosperous, with modern building developments spreading over the surrounding countryside.

15

The Three Beiras

The area across the width of the country south of the Douro is in three sections: Beira Litoral (Coastal Beira), Beira Alta (Upper Beira), and Beira Baixa (Lower Beira).

The Beira Litoral is roughly L-shaped, with its longest side down the Atlantic coast. It is a low-lying region, with sand dunes, salt marshes, and rice fields by the sea, while farther inland wheat and corn grow on small farms. There are also orchards, olive groves, and vineyards. The main

The university library at Coimbra. This ornate Baroque masterpiece was completed in 1728. The portrait at the end of the vista is of King João V, who commissioned the work. Exotic woods, especially ebony from the Portuguese colony of Brazil, were used for the decorative carving, which was then lavishly gilded.

town is Coimbra. Until 1260, it was the capital of Portugal, and it has the country's oldest university, founded in 1307. Close by, at Conimbriga, a Roman town has been excavated.

The Beira Alta and the eastern part of Beira Baixa are mountainous, sharing mainland Portugal's highest mountain range, the Serra da Estrela, between them. Its main peak, the Torre, 6,539 feet (1,993 meters), is only surpassed by the Pico 7,611 feet (2,320 meters) in the Azores. The Serra da Estrela's summits are snow-covered in winter. Birch trees grow below the snow line, while the lower slopes are forested with pine and chestnut trees. Most of the people in this region live along the beautiful valleys of the Mondego and Zêzere rivers.

Estremadura

Estremadura is a rather long, narrow province lying beside the Atlantic, south of the Beira

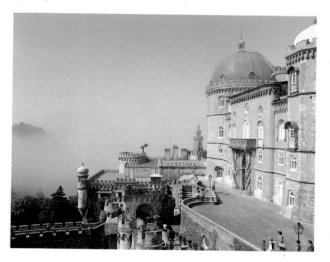

The Palácio da Pena, on a hilltop outside the town of Sintra, west of Lisbon. It was begun in 1840 for King Ferdinand II and is just one of several fanciful mock-Gothic castles that were built in Europe around the same time.

Litoral, and is dominated by Lisbon, the capital.

The coast is dotted with fishing villages, sandy beaches, and cliffs. Inland the rolling countryside is cultivated intensively. The whole province has a settled, comfortable air about it, mainly because most of it is within easy reach of Lisbon, which makes it a favorite area for commuters to the big city.

Several of the main towns grew up around monasteries and palaces. Alcobaça surrounds a huge medieval monastery where as many as 999 monks once lived. Sintra has two palaces and many large gardens hidden by high walls. Obidos has a magnificent hilltop castle.

The coast turns eastward to the mouth of the Tagus and is lined with prosperous houses and hotels all the way to Lisbon. South of Lisbon, across the river, is the Setúbal peninsula, with the hilly Serra da Arrábida as its spine. This limestone range has more than a thousand species of plants, with lovely displays of wild flowers in the spring. The main town here is Setúbal, Portugal's third largest, with its dockyard and industries, which include fish canneries, a car assembly plant, and salt pans where salt has been created for centuries by evaporating sea water.

The Ribatejo

The Ribatejo, whose name means "the bank of the Tagus," lies east of Estremadura, on a plain of rich soil. Intensive irrigation with water from the river allows rice to be grown. Wheat, millet, and vegetables are farmed here too, and the wide grasslands are home to horses and black bulls. The powerful crusading order of the Knights

The monastery of Tomar has some fine examples of the flamboyant decoration called Manueline, after King Manuel I. This great window at Tomar (1510) is surrounded by marine symbols to commemorate the Age of Discoveries. At the top is the Cross of the Order of Christ, which decorated the sails of the exploring ships. Twined around the frame are ropes, anchor chains, coral, and seaweed.

Templar built a great monastery at Tomar. It was later the headquarters of the Order of Christ, which was closely involved with the explorations of Henry the Navigator. Its red cross symbol was carried on the sails of his ships.

The Alentejo

The Alentejo is really two provinces, Alto and Baixo Alentejo. They take up approximately 30 percent of Portugal's total area. The name means "beyond the Tagus," viewed from the north, as the Christians did when it was occupied by the Moors.

The Alentejo is a huge, flat plain, covered by fields of wheat and groves of oak and olive trees. Flocks of sheep and goats graze the sparse grasslands where more intensive agriculture is not possible. Herds of black pigs feed on fallen acorns under the oak trees and provide Portugal with pork, its favorite meat.

The Algarve

This is Portugal's vacation province, often the only part of the country that visitors from abroad see. Its name is Arabic and comes from *el-gharb*, meaning "the west," as it was the westernmost point the Moors managed to reach in their conquest of the Iberian Peninsula.

The Algarve lies across the southern border of the Alentejo, separated from it by a range of low hills in the east, the Serra do Caldeirão, and the granite, forested Serra de Mochique in the west. It is a province of fruit trees, sandy beaches dotted with weirdly shaped rocks, flat-roofed houses topped by fancy chimneys, gardens bright with

The rocks on the Algarve coast have been worn into fanciful forms by ages of wind and weather. It is fun to take a boat trip into the hidden coves and see the rock shapes towering overhead. These rocks are at Ponta da Piedade, near Lagos.

flowers, huge tourist hotels, and spreading suburban development. Along the coast there are busy local fishing fleets. The extreme western point is Cabo de São Vincente (Cape St. Vincent), the most southwesterly point of the European continent.

The Azores

The Azores islands are formed from submerged volcanoes with just the peaks showing above the ocean. Like Madeira, the name was given by the first discoverers. *Ihlas dos Açores* means Islands of the Hawks. The nine islands are in three groups, with São Miguel, the largest island, in the most southeasterly one.

The old craters are now lakes, surrounded by greenery. The islands are not quite so luxuriant as

Caldeira das Sete Cidades (Cauldron of the Seven Cities) on the island of São Miguel, in the Azores. It is a chain of three lakes filling the crater of an extinct volcano. Seven towns were supposed to have been drowned when the lakes were formed.

Madeira but still have plenty of trees, such as pines, chestnuts, and bamboos. The climate is subtropical, windy and warm, with plenty of rain. The islands have almost no industry but good agriculture. Islanders grow grain, fruit, tea, and tobacco for export. Fish are plentiful in the open Atlantic waters around the coasts.

The population for the whole archipelago is 254,200, and just over half live on São Miguel, whose chief town is also the archipelago's capital, Ponta Delgada.

The Lost Kingdom of Atlantis
Legend has it that Madeira and the Azores were part of the lost realm of Atlantis. Madeira was first discovered in 1419, uninhabited and covered with dense forest. The Portuguese called it *Ilha da Madeira*, which means "island of timber."

Madeira

Madeira is one of a group of islands formed by the tops of submerged, extinct volcanoes. There are ten islands in the group, two of which are little better than rocks. On Madeira, green, tropically lush, terraced slopes rise up the steep sides of the mountains, with flowers everywhere. Almost one third of the rocky island can be cultivated, with sugarcane as one of the main crops. The volcanic soil is ideal for growing grapes, and the island makes a wine that is also called madeira.

The capital, Funchal, stands on a bay. About one third of the island's population of 271,400 lives in and around it. In its early days Funchal was sometimes attacked by pirates for the treasures of its rich churches and houses. In the center of the island, hidden in an old volcanic crater 3,366 feet (1,026 meters) up, is Curral das Freiras, where the nuns from an early convent used to take refuge when the town was in danger.

3 Portugal's Early History

Portugal became a separate country in 1139. Until then it was just the westernmost part of the Iberian Peninsula, sharing its history with Spain.

It had been inhabited since the very earliest times. The Ice Ages left Portugal almost untouched, and wanderers settled in its warm climate, living mainly along the rivers and the seashore. Tribes from across the Pyrenees migrated into the Iberian Peninsula for several thousand years during the Neolithic, Copper, and Bronze Ages, bringing their culture and crafts with them. Celts, with their skills in working iron, began to drift into the area a thousand years before the time of Christ.

In the 800s B.C. the Phoenicians, from the eastern Mediterranean, set up trading posts around the coast. The Phoenicians were wandering merchants who roamed the seas around Europe in search of outlets for their merchandise. They bartered for local raw materials, especially copper, tin, and amber. Their trading posts were located as far north as Tintagel in Cornwall, England, and in Scandinavia. In Portugal, they settled at the mouth of the Tagus, where the river gave easy access to the interior.

The next arrivals were the Greeks and the Carthaginians. The Carthaginians came from North Africa, where Tunisia is today. By 535 B.C. they had taken over from the Phoenicians, to whom they were related, and proceeded to exploit the mineral resources of the peninsula, mining gold, tin, and copper. Then beginning in 260 B.C. the Carthaginians waged a series of wars with Rome, called the Punic Wars, to decide who would rule the Mediterranean. The Romans won and tried to wipe all traces of their enemy from the face of the Earth.

Roman remains at Conimbriga. This partially reconstructed Roman villa shows the layout of the central courtyard with its surrounding elaborate mosaic pavement. Conimbriga was founded by the Romans in the second century B.C. and finally destroyed in A.D. 468.

The Romans

The Romans took over from the Carthaginians in the Iberian Peninsula in 137 B.C. They called the province Lusitania after the Lusitani, a warrior tribe that lived in the area between the Douro and the Tagus. Lusitania became a valuable addition to the Roman Empire, providing salt, wheat, and copper for the ready markets of Italy. Just as important as these were the local men who joined

> **Roman Remains**
> Substantial remains of the Roman occupation can be seen around the country. Their solid bridges are still in use. Stretches of their roads and sections of aqueducts dot the countryside. In the center of Évora (which the Romans called Ebora) there is a columned temple to the Roman goddess Diana. Excavations at Conimbriga (Condeixa), near Coimbra, have revealed the remains of a major Roman settlement, with mosaic pavements and the foundations of villas.

the Roman legions as Lusitanian recruits.

In their usual efficient way, the Romans began to put their new colony in order. They created small fortified towns all over the province. Julius Caesar used one of them, Olissipo (now called Lisbon), as his administrative center. The Romans had to subdue the rebellious tribes as they proceeded. To facilitate the passage of troops and thus strengthen their grip on the country, they linked their strongholds together by a network of durable roads. The main one ran from north to south, roughly parallel to the coast.

The Suevi and Visigoths

Conimbriga had to be fortified when the Barbarians from northern Europe attacked across the Pyrenees in A.D. 260. Stone was in short supply, and hastily broken-up chunks of statues and sections of columns can still be seen embedded in the defensive walls. Although the Barbarians did not get as far as Lusitania that time, they were the forerunners of further waves of invaders that finally took over the whole Iberian Peninsula.

Beginning about A.D. 411, there was a series of invasions by tribes from northern Europe, but only the Suevi (Swabians) and the Visigoths settled permanently. The Swabians were a German tribe whose warriors Julius Caesar had respected as fighters. Now, four centuries after his time, they put down roots far from their original German homeland and occupied the northwest corner of the Iberian Peninsula, about a quarter of the whole territory.

The Visigoths originally had been allies of the Romans, and their strength had waxed as Rome's power waned. At first they controlled the remaining three quarters of the peninsula, but in A.D. 585 the Visigothic king, Leovigild, took over the whole country. By this time the people of the peninsula had all been converted to Christianity.

Rule by the Moors

After the death of Muhammad in A.D. 632, the religion of Islam, which he founded, had spread outward from its birthplace beside the Arabian Gulf, carried by conquering Muslim armies. By the end of the century they had occupied the whole of North Africa right up to Morocco, just eight miles across the Straits of Gibraltar from the Iberian Peninsula.

In the spring of A.D. 711 a pretender to the Visigothic throne was trying to get help to take over the throne. He made the serious mistake of calling on the Muslims for military aid. The invitation to cross the narrow channel of the

Straits of Gibraltar was just the opportunity that the Moors had been waiting for. It gave them the chance to carry their faith into western Europe. Within two years they were in possession of the southern half of the Iberian Peninsula. In another two years they had a hold on most of the rest.

The conquered Christians began gradually to organize themselves and fight back. It was to take them five hundred years to drive the Moors out, in a long series of campaigns that became known as the Reconquest. Although it was fought on home soil, to the Christian warriors the Reconquest was a crusade, a holy war against the infidel, just as much as the crusades that were being fought for the Holy Land itself.

The north of what is now Portugal put up some of the strongest resistance to the Muslims. By A.D. 868 the Christian forces had regained the land down to the Douro and were able to occupy and rebuild the city of Portucale (Oporto). The area between the Minho and Douro rivers took its name from the town and was known in Latin as *Territorium Portugalense*. In 1139 this territory became a small kingdom separate from Spain, with Dom Afonso Henriques as its first king, Afonso I. He pushed the border farther south and recaptured Lisbon in 1147, but it took over a century for the Reconquest of Portugal to be completed. Faro was taken in 1249, and the Moors were finally driven from the Algarve.

The age of the great discoveries

Afonso I belonged to the House of Burgundy, which ruled Portugal until 1383. In that year, the first king of the House of Aviz, João I, won a major victory over the Spanish at Aljubarrota. This resulted in Portugal being safe from invasion for the next 200 years.

English soldiers helped the Portuguese to drive out the Moors, and 500 crossbowmen fought with the Portuguese at Aljubarrota. In 1386, Portugal signed a pact of friendship with England, the Treaty of Windsor. It was the first of many that were signed over the centuries, but a very important one. To seal the alliance, the next year João I married the English princess Philippa of Lancaster, daughter of John of Gaunt. Her brother became Henry IV of England.

Another Henry, one of the five sons of João and Philippa, began Portugal's overseas exploration. He always spent money lavishly and was imaginative enough to seek extra sources of income overseas. He financed the ships that discovered Madeira in 1419. The Azores were first

Part of the Monument to the Discoveries, erected in 1960 on the 500th anniversary of the death of Prince Henry the Navigator. This memorial stands beside the mouth of the Tagus River, at Belém, just outside Lisbon. Henry is poised as if on the prow of a ship, looking seaward, and holding a model of a caravel, one of his ships.

The Battle of Aljubarrota

On August 14, 1385, late in the afternoon of an extremely hot and dusty day, the armies of Spain and Portugal met in battle to decide who should rule Portugal.

The Spanish army was led by the Castilian king, Juan I, and consisted of 30,000 men. The Portuguese forces were led by Dom Jão of Aviz, an illegitimate half-brother of the recently deceased Portuguese king. Both he and his general, Nun' Alvares Pereira, were only 20 at the time. Their army was 7,000 strong. Five hundred of the soldiers were English bowmen famous for the accuracy of their archery.

King Juan, who was ill, was riding a donkey. He ordered his nobles not to attack the Portuguese, but the hotheaded officers disobeyed his orders and launched a series of haphazard raids. The battle lasted an hour, for when the Castilian banner was captured the Spanish troops fled, led by Juan on his donkey. João claimed that 2,500 enemy soldiers had been killed, as well as many Portuguese nobles who had chosen to support Juan instead of him.

Although the battle was over quickly, its effects were long lasting. Portugal had established a right to freedom from Spanish rule that lasted for the next 200 years.

Before the battle Dom João had sworn an oath that if he won he would build the most beautiful abbey imaginable to be dedicated to the Virgin Mary. The legend says that after the battle the king hurled his spear into the air saying he would build where it landed. The king must have had quite an arm, as the great abbey of Battalha (Battle Abbey) was built 10 miles (16 kilometers) from the battlefield.

visited in 1427 and colonized in 1445. To provide experienced seamen for his explorations, he opened a school in Sagres, in the Algarve, where sailors were instructed in navigation. From this he earned the nickname "Prince Henry the Navigator." Henry's ships, called *caravels*, sailed down the west coast of Africa annually from 1434 to 1436, going a little farther each year. Wearing a broad-brimmed hat to shield himself from the fierce Algarve sun, Henry the Navigator became a legendary figure. His instructions in the use of navigation by the stars made it possible for explorers to cover great distances out of sight of land with much greater accuracy.

Further discoveries

The explorations of the Age of Discoveries continued after Henry died in 1460. In 1487, Bartolomeu Dias sailed around the Cape of Good Hope, at the southern tip of Africa, trying to find a new sea route to India. Ten years later Vasco da Gama spent two years completing the exploration of that route, returning in 1499 with his ship's hold full of pepper, cloves, cinnamon, nutmeg, and precious stones. In those days before refrigeration, spices were almost as valuable as gems. They could be used to disguise the flavor of poor meat, or meat that had been cured or salted to preserve it through the winter. Portugal established a colony at Goa on the west coast of India and took over the trade routes from India to Europe.

Portugal had refused to finance Columbus, who was married to a Portuguese sea captain's daughter, in his attempt to find a way to the Indies by sailing due west. Instead Spain gave Columbus the money, which was greatly to its advantage when Columbus reached America in 1492, believing that he had found a new route to India. In 1494, the treaty of Tordesillas between Spain and Portugal, signed at a small town just over the border in Spain, confirmed Portugal's right to explore the sea route to the East Indies and to lay claim to lands east of a line running north and south through the bulge of South America. This meant that Portugal was able to claim the rich country of Brazil, which was visited in 1500 by Pedro Alvares Cabral.

Portuguese mariners in the North Atlantic explored Greenland, Newfoundland, Nova Scotia, and Labrador. Labrador is named after its discoverer, João Fernandes, whose nickname was O Lavrador, "the farmer."

In 1519, a Portuguese sea captain, Fernando de Megalhães, known today as Magellan, set sail in a Spanish ship. He passed through the straits off the southern tip of South America, which are now named after him, and crossed the Pacific. He was killed in the Philippines, but his companions were the first to sail around the world, arriving home in 1522.

These voyages, which completed the discovery of parts of the world that had been unknown to Europeans until then, took almost exactly a century. Their effect on the nation of Portugal was tremendous. Manuel I, who ruled from 1495 to 1521, and whose arms were so long that his hands reached to his knees, became the richest king in all of Europe.

4

Invasions by Spain and France

This castle at Marvão was built in the 1200s to defend Portugal's border with Spain. It stands high on a crag 2,838 feet (865 meters) up, with a medieval village clustered below. The surrounding walls give strategic views over the countryside. A cistern within the keep could hold six months' supply of water. This almost impregnable stronghold was still in use in the 1830s.

Although Portugal was often threatened by the Spanish over the centuries that followed the battle of Aljubarrota in 1385, it was occupied by them only once. In 1530, the king of Spain and the king of Portugal had married each other's sister. This meant that 50 years later, when the last legitimate male of the ruling Portuguese House of Aviz died, Philip II of Spain could claim the empty Portuguese throne to become Philip I of Portugal. He, his son, and his grandson (both also called Philip), ruled Portugal from 1580 to 1640.

Philip II of Spain and I of Portugal (1527 - 98). All his life Philip supported the efforts of the Roman Catholic Church to destroy Protestantism. He married Mary I of England (known as Bloody Mary) in 1554, and together they tried unsuccessfully to restore Catholicism to England. After he had added Portugal to the Spanish crown, he launched the Armada to try to topple Mary's successor, Elizabeth I, from her Protestant throne.

TEATRO BELGICO,

Philip I started to plan the invasion of England soon after he took over the Portuguese throne. He dragged an unwilling Portugal, still a firm ally of England, into his schemes. Thirty-one of the 146 ships of the ill-fated Spanish Armada were built in the Lisbon dockyards and sailed from there in 1588. The Armada was routed by a combination of bad weather and the English fleet. Few of the Portuguese ships returned.

Philip interfered very little with Portugal's internal affairs, although he did strengthen the fearful Inquisition. His son and grandson were not very interested in Portugal, and during their reign Spain took Portuguese money and men to support itself in endless foreign wars.

The Portuguese Inquisition

At one time, Portugal was regarded with horror by most of Europe for the ferocity of the way the Inquisition was carried out there. The Inquisition was established as a religious law court by the Catholic Church in the 1230s to make sure that people followed the Church's rules and beliefs. Those who didn't were called heretics and punished, often by death. In Portugal, the heretics were mainly new Christians—Jews or Muslims who had been converted to Christianity. There were thousands of them, and they formed a wealthy middle class.

In Portugal, the Inquisition, greedy for wealth and power, went way beyond its religious role. In fact, from 1580 to 1640 when the country was joined to Spain, the Inquisition practically ran Portugal. It had a huge bureaucracy and almost unlimited authority throughout the country and its colonies. It maintained a secret force of spies and informers (*familiares*) who betrayed their fellow citizens. The Inquisition was even able to search ships in harbor for books and papers with which it disagreed.

At the height of its power, between 1543 and 1684, 1,379 people were burned at the stake in public executions (*autos da fé*). Sometimes the victims were chained to iron chairs and roasted to death. After 1684, the Inquisition's power declined, though it was not until 1761 that its last victim, a Jesuit priest, died. It was finally disbanded in 1769.

The desire for freedom from Spain grew in Portugal until, in 1640, when Spain's attention was concentrated on trying to subdue a revolt in Catalonia, Portugal declared itself independent.

A distant relative of the former royal house of Portugal and the largest landowner in the country, the Duke of Braganza, was declared king as João IV. He was crowned in an outdoor ceremony in Lisbon, just before Christmas 1640. In 1661, England renewed its friendship with Portugal by another treaty. The treaty was reinforced by the marriage of Charles II to Catherine, the daughter of João IV, who is known as Catherine of Braganza. Spain finally recognized Portugal's independence in 1668.

Napoleon
Although Portugal's geographical position has kept it out of European conflicts during almost all of its history, it could not escape the greed of Napoleon. Faithful to its long friendship with England, Portugal had been anti-French during the French Revolution. It refused to support Napoleon when he came to power and tried to blockade Britain. In 1807, after concluding a treaty with Spain, Napoleon's general Andoche Junot was able to march his troops through Spain to occupy Portugal. The Portuguese royal family fled to Brazil for safety, sailing in British ships.

In 1808, British troops under the command of General Arthur Wellesley (later the Duke of Wellington) landed in Portugal. For three years Portuguese and British soldiers fought together to drive the French out of the country. They succeeded twice, although the French returned each time.

In 1809, Wellesley secretly constructed the Lines of Torres Vedras, a chain of 152 strong points situated on hilltops north of Lisbon, to

The Lines of Torres Vedras during the Peninsula Campaign, with the French troops and the British in close conflict.

defend the capital. In 1810, the French general, André Masséna, discovered the fortifications and, not knowing just how strong they were, waited for five months for reinforcements to arrive before daring to attack. He gave up in early March 1811, and retreated, first into Spain, then into France, harassed along the way by the allied troops. It was the beginning of a change in Napoleon's fortunes. He was finally defeated at the battle of Waterloo in 1815.

The Portuguese royal family did not return from Brazil until 1821, after the country achieved independence from Portugal.

5

Into the Twentieth Century

One of the results for Portugal of Napoleon's invasion was that it lost control of most of its overseas trade, especially with Brazil. When this source of wealth was seriously cut back, the country's economy started a slow slide into debt. This decline spread over the following decades, with total financial collapse a continual threat.

The royal family had so enjoyed life in Brazil, which had been made a kingdom equal to Portugal in 1815, that they were undecided whether they should base themselves in Brazil or in Portugal.

Almost a century after Napoleon's defeat, in 1908, after a long series of weak rulers had failed to solve the country's problems, the king and his eldest son were shot dead in a Lisbon square. The king's young son, Manuel II, who was wounded in the same attack, came to the throne but ruled for only two years. In 1910, he fled to England, where he lived until his death in 1932. Portugal's days as a monarchy were over. Chaos followed. There were 45 governments between 1910 and 1926. The country was bankrupt and the escudo became almost worthless.

The Salazar years

In 1928, in an attempt to solve Portugal's crippling financial problems, Dr. António de Oliveira Salazar, a professor of economics at Coimbra University, was appointed minister of finance. By

Dr. António de Oliveira Salazar (1889–1970), dictator of Portugal. This photograph was taken in 1954 when he was at the height of his power.

introducing strict accounting systems, cutting down expenditures, and enforcing new taxes, he was able to convert the massive national debt into a surplus in a single year. In 1932, he became prime minister and almost immediately began to exercise power as a complete dictator. In 1933, his *Estado Novo* (New State) policy banned trade unions, industrial strikes, and political parties. A secret police force, the PIDE, made sure that there could be no opposition to his rule. The PIDE used torture, prisons, and even concentration camps to gain its ends. The police were supplied with information by thousands of informers, many of them very poor, who betrayed their friends and relations for pay. Salazar was very proud that he kept Portugal free from debt and had made the streets peaceful and safe. He did it, however, by sentencing the country to 40 years of stagnation during which it became one of the most backward countries in Europe.

Colonial revolt

Portugal was neutral during World War II, taking sides with neither the Allies nor the German

Angola, on the west coast of Africa, was a Portuguese colony for at least four centuries. The Angola civil war started in 1961 and lasted for 14 years. Here a Portuguese army patrol, with guns at the ready, is searching a jungle area in the early 1970s. The unpopular war ended in 1975 when Angola was granted its independence.

Axis, although Salazar's sympathies were with the Germans. Lisbon and its nearby fashionable coastal resorts became a meeting point for spies and refugees from Hitler's occupation of the rest of Europe. Neutrality was a policy that paid off. After the war was over, Salazar had gathered enough financial credit to be able to start a modest modernization of the country's economy. Many

Under Portuguese Administration

Macao is a small peninsula (6 square miles, 15.5 square kilometers), on the coast of China. It lies 45 miles (70 kilometers) southwest of Hong Kong. The Portuguese arrived there to set up a trading post in 1516, during the period of their voyages of exploration. They obtained a lease of the peninsula from China in 1557. Macao (which is called Macau in Portuguese and *An Men* in Chinese) will be returned to China on December 20, 1999. The colony has run its own internal affairs since 1976, although the governor is still appointed by Portugal. It has a population of about half a million, 95 percent of whom are Chinese.

Macao is quite wealthy, producing textiles (especially embroidered material), fireworks, and electronic goods, and has a flourishing tourist industry. It is popular for a day or weekend trip from nearby Hong Kong, by those who want to get away from the huge crowds there and enjoy the quieter life of the peninsula, eat its excellent Portuguese cooking, and spend their money in its enticing shops.

Most of Macao is developed, but there are two smaller islands, Taipa and Coloane, connected to Macao by bridges, with some open country and sandy beaches.

European nations owed Portugal millions when the war ended. Salazar began to build roads, bridges, and hydroelectric dams to supply power to make up for the lack of other sources of fuel. Portugal's industry grew at the rate of a healthy nine percent a year during the 1950s and 1960s.

Portugal, however, had African colonies, and its greedy policies there were often condemned by the United Nations. In the early 1960s, the colonies of Angola, Portuguese Guinea (now Guinea-Bissau), and Mozambique began to revolt against Salazar's rule. To try to suppress the colonial independence movements, more and more Portuguese soldiers were sent to Africa. By 1968, there were over 100,000 of them there, waging a war that Portugal could ill afford.

The revolution and after
In 1968, Salazar, who was then 79, fell out of a deck chair and suffered a brain hemorrhage. The stroke left him paralyzed, and he died in 1970. He was replaced as prime minister in 1968 by Marcello Caetano, a professor of law. Caetano relaxed Salazar's repressive policies a little but continued the increasingly unpopular and costly war against the guerrillas in Africa. Within the army a group calling itself the Armed Forces Movement (MFA) decided to act. On April 25, 1974, they seized power in Portugal. It was a bloodless coup, called the Carnation Revolution because of the flowers that students and civilians put in the barrels of the soldiers' rifles.

Among the early acts of the new military regime was the granting of independence to the African colonies. Over 750,000 Portuguese

Soldiers are cheered on the streets of Lisbon on the day of the Carnation Revolution, April 25, 1974. It was on this day that the army staged the coup that freed Portugal from dictatorship and introduced an era of growing democracy.

settlers chose to return to Portugal, having lost their African homes. These refugees (*retornados*) arrived in a country putting socialism into practice. Banks and industry had been nationalized. Four million acres of land, mainly on large estates, were seized from the owners and distributed to the farm workers. The hated secret police force was disbanded.

These extreme left-wing policies almost caused a civil war in 1975. It was averted when a new constitution was drawn up in 1976, which took

43

power from the army and gave it to the Assembly. The constitution was followed by elections, and very slowly the Portuguese turned away from a situation that could have brought a civil conflict. The less practical socialist measures were gradually reversed, and Portugal began to put itself onto a firm economic and democratic basis.

In 1986, Portugal joined the European Community together with its neighbor, Spain, and entered on a prosperous new phase in its history.

The government

Portugal is a republic, a parliamentary state ruled by an Assembly, elected every four years. The Assembly has 250 seats, with four reserved for Portuguese citizens living abroad. This odd provision is partly in recognition of the importance to the economy of those who are the source of so much foreign currency. It was recently estimated that the number of Portuguese living out of the country was just under four million.

The head of state is the president, who is elected for a five-year term. The leader of the government is the prime minister, appointed by the president, who normally chooses the leader of the party with the most votes. The president has the power to dissolve the Assembly anytime except during the first six months of a new Assembly or during the last six months of his own term of office.

Portugal is divided into 22 administrative districts, 18 in mainland Portugal, four in Madeira and the Azores.

6 Lisbon

The capital of Portugal is Lisbon (Lisboa in Portuguese). It stands on the northern bank of the wide estuary of the Tagus River, called the "Sea of Straw," supposedly because the sun's reflections seem to turn it a rippling yellow. This was the obvious place to build a town from very early times. The river estuary made an excellent natural harbor, and there was a convenient hill beside it on which protective defenses could be built. The excellent harbor has been the chief reason for Lisbon's prosperity for three thousand years.

The center of Lisbon is full of colorfully painted old buildings. Steep streets climb between them, crowded with people and noisy with clattering

Praça Dom Pedro IV, known as The Rossio. This square is the heart of Lisbon. In the center stands a column with a bronze statue of King Pedro IV at the top (seen here from the back). He reigned for just two years (1836-38) but managed to win a civil war during that time. The gray-and-white patterned pavement, made of cut stones, was laid in the mid-1800s by convicts.

streetcars. Everywhere the walls are plastered with posters and grafitti, mostly about political matters. Some of the sidewalks and main squares in the old sections of the city are paved with square gray and white cobblestones, set in a wavy pattern.

Modern Lisbon begins outside the ancient city center, spreading over the surrounding hills, with miles of new apartment buildings and housing developments. It has also swallowed up the small towns and villages around its edge, especially those that stretch westward along the coast to Estoril and Cascais.

Lisbon is not only a busy port but the headquarters of the government. Major roads and railroad lines radiate outward from the city, and it has the country's main airport. In recent

A modern low-cost housing development at Queluz. The suburbs of Lisbon have been choked by similar nondescript high-rise apartment buildings in the last 20 years.

years, the fast-developing northern city of Oporto has drawn a lot of business and industrial life away from Lisbon, but a great deal still remains.

Lisbon's history

The Phoenicians founded Lisbon around 1200 B.C. and gave the settlement the name Olissipo. They were traders from the eastern Mediterranean, who saw this as a perfect place to set up a successful trading post.

The Lisbon Earthquake

On the morning of November 1, 1755, the city suffered a terrible earthquake, whose tremors were felt as far away as Switzerland and the Scilly Isles in Britain. The subsequent tidal wave engulfed ships lying at anchor and swamped the low-lying parts of the city. Overturned candles and cooking stoves caused fires that raged through the city for nearly a week, completing the terrible damage started by the earthquake and the tidal wave. Many of the city's riches, its libraries, paintings, and beautiful churches, were wiped out. Between 10,000 and 15,000 people were killed. The city center by the river was largely destroyed.

The king's chief minister, the Marquis de Pombal, who had been the Portuguese ambassador to London, set about restoring order among the demoralized townsfolk and took charge of reconstructing the shattered city. He had the devastated center rebuilt on a grid pattern, with straight, wide streets and severely plain buildings, a revolutionary concept for its period. This area, called the Baixa, became the business center of Lisbon.

The Phoenicians were followed by the Greeks and the Carthaginians. The Romans arrived in 205 B.C., after conquering the Carthaginians. They built their town on and around the hill where the castle of São Jorge (St. George) now stands. The next invaders to leave their mark on Lisbon were the Moors, followers of Islam from North Africa, who created a Moorish citadel where the Roman fort had stood.

During the centuries that followed the expulsion of the Moors in 1147, wealth from Portugal's overseas explorations flowed into the country. Lisbon, the center of most of the trade in spices from the East, gold, and gems, grew to become one of the richest and most beautiful cities in Europe.

Some places of interest

One part of Lisbon that escaped the new city planning after the 1755 earthquake was the Alfama, an ancient warren of narrow lanes that climbs up from the river to the castle. It got its name from the Moors who had public bath houses (*al hamma* means "bath" in Arabic). At one side of the Alfama is the old cathedral, which is built like a fortress itself. There are panoramic views over the city and the river from São Jorge's battlements. White peacocks, black swans, and turkeys roam the gardens that lie within the castle's now ruined walls.

West of the castle stands another hill called Bairro Alto. Beside the Rossio square there is a tall wrought-iron tower, the Elevador de Santa Justa. It looks like a miniature Eiffel Tower and contains an elevator that is the easy way of getting up the

Public gardens opposite the Jerónimos Monastery, outside Lisbon. The Portuguese love gardens, a taste that they may have inherited from the Moorish invaders. The use of pools and fountains was a trademark of the Moors, a desert people who enjoyed the cooling sound of tinkling water in a hot climate.

hill. Like Greenwich Village in New York and the Left Bank in Paris, the Bairro Alto used to be the artistic part of town where writers and painters once lived. Its streets are full of tall houses with balconies and it contains Lisbon's most elegant shopping district. Unfortunately, a fire in 1988 destroyed part of this neighborhood, and with it many of the stores. Most of the front walls were saved, so that rebuilding can go on behind these façades and recreate the appearance of the area before the fire.

The Lisbon opera house, Teatro de São Carlos, built in 1792, is here. So, too, is the Convento do Carmo, the spectacular remains of a great church belonging to the Carmelite monks, which was finally finished in 1423. In the earthquake of 1755,

49

The great cloisters of the Jerónimos Monastery. The vast wealth of the spice trade flowed into Portugal in the reign of King Manuel I and helped to pay for this magnificent building, built mainly between 1502 and 1522. The lower level of these cloisters has a small jungle of carvings, with all sorts of faces, human and animal, peering out from between sculpted plants.

the church lost its roof and has remained largely open to the sky ever since. Today, there is an archaeological museum in the ruins, with pieces of sculpture, tiles, and ceramics from all over Portugal.

The long, wide Avenida da Liberdade, Liberty Avenue, runs northward through the center of town, with trees, statues, and fountains along its length. At the top of the avenue is a park named after King Edward VII of England, and beside this park is a disused limestone quarry, which has been converted into an indoor fairytale garden called the Estufa Fria. There are waterfalls, pools, and ferns, splashed with the flaming colors of orchids, red poinsettias, and purple fuchsias. All this luxuriant foliage is interlaced with rocky steps and high, narrow paths. It is a refreshingly cool, shady place to visit after the hot sun outside.

West of the city, at Belém (a local way of saying Bethlehem), stands the riverside Jerónimos Monastery. It was from this spot, in 1497, that Vasco da Gama sailed in the hope of discovering the sea route to India. The magnificent monastery was built in thanks for his successful voyage. Its construction was financed by a five percent tax on the spices, gems, and gold that poured into the country as a result of the new trade route.

Right on the river's edge is the Torre de Belém (Belém Tower), a small, elaborate fort built to guard the harbor. Beside it is the modern Monument to the Discoveries, carved out of white stone, which commemorates Portugal's great overseas explorations. It is designed to look like a huge sailing ship's prow, with a statue of Prince Henry the Navigator poised, looking out over the river.

7

Portugal's Economy and Industries

Two events in recent years have started to change Portugal from a sleepy, backward country to a bustling, modern one. The first was the 1974 revolution, which ended the 45 years of dictatorship in which the country seemed to be marking time. The second was when Portugal joined the European Community (EC) in 1986.

One of the poorest countries in Europe, Portugal suddenly began to receive billions of escudos in EC subsidies and loans, designed to help overhaul and modernize every part of its way of life. Portugal now receives more financial

Marble is one of Portugal's valuable exports. These marble works at Pero-Penheiro, near Sintra, are close to quarries from which pink marble is cut. It is very popular for use in decorating Portuguese churches.

Privatization

Today many believe that banks and industries in private hands are better able to adjust to a changing financial climate than rigidly state-controlled ones can. Businesses that were nationalized immediately after the revolution are being returned to the private sector. This return to privatization started in 1989 and immediately began to show results. At first firms were allowed to have only 49 percent private ownership, with the government keeping a controlling 51 percent. In February 1990, a new law was passed that permitted corporations to be 100 percent privately owned.

The Portuguese government may well be losing money by this policy. Although it was estimated that in 1990 the profit to the state from selling off its interests to the private sector would be 158 billion escudos, the old debts that the government has had to write off could add up to much more. However, in the long run the state will benefit. Any debts that companies may incur will not have to be borne by the government.

aid per person than any other EC country. For example, during the years 1990 to 1993, it will be spending 450 billion escudos on the training of much-needed professionals, such as doctors, engineers, and teachers. The European Social Fund will supply 290 billion escudos. In 1989, huge sums of money were invested in Portugal by other countries. Britain, France, and Spain topped the list of contributors. Britain invested about $450 million, mainly in property, tourism, and banking; France the equivalent of $265 million, mainly in property and manufacturing; and Spain the equivalent of $260 million, mainly in banking and property.

The "rags to riches" nature of these changes has brought problems, too. So vast has been the tidal wave of finance flowing in that the old-fashioned economy of Portugal has found it difficult to absorb it all and to spend it sensibly. To deal with so much money Portugal has had to take radical steps to make the nation's economy much more flexible than it was in the past.

Resources
One of the factors in Portugal's slow development has been its relative lack of fuel and mineral resources. Portugal has very little coal, although there are deposits of the soft brown coal, lignite. No exploitable oil or natural gas has been located either on- or off-shore. To compensate for its lack of accessible fuel, Portugal has recently invested widely in hydroelectric power. Rivers in the north have been dammed, some of the work being done in collaboration with Spain because the rivers flow through both countries. The hydroelectric projects underway on the Douro River, which rises in Spain and forms part of the border of the two countries, are also financed by both countries. Eventually the power produced by damming the Douro and its tributaries will provide electricity for most of Portugal's needs.

Portugal does have a variety of other mineral deposits, although not generally large quantities of any single one. Among the most valuable is wolframite, the ore from which tungsten is

Modern Portuguese industry relies on cheap electricity from hydroelectric programs. This dam across the Zêzere River, a tributary of the Douro, is one of a chain of dams in the area. A nearby reservoir supplies Lisbon with some of its drinking water.

obtained. Tungsten is used in the making of high-grade steel. Portugal also has the second largest deposits of uranium in Europe. In addition there are deposits of lead, zinc, manganese, and cuprous iron pyrites. Rock salt, marble, slate, and granite are also mined and exported.

Wages and working conditions

Despite the recent changes in the Portuguese economy, wages and working conditions still have a long way to go to catch up with other European countries. In early 1990 in Portugal, the minimum legal wage in industry was increased to 35,000 escudos per month, the equivalent of a weekly wage of about $60 in the United States. At that time union wage settlements were running

Ribatejo cowboys rounding up cattle. Like many modern cowboys, Portuguese cowpokes ride motorcycles as well as horses.

even below this already extremely low figure.

Unemployment was more than five percent early in 1990, and the constantly changing economic conditions made layoffs fairly common. Working conditions, too, could be very harsh, especially in the poorer north of the country.

Partly because of an earlier shortage of money, Portugal has experienced delays in benefiting from technological advances. Agriculture represents a good example of this problem. In addition to the earlier lack of money to fund more up-to-date farming methods, Portugal's small farms do not lend themselves to the use of large, modern farm machinery. There is also a certain amount of difficulty in changing some out-of-date attitudes toward farming. However, there is a very active national Young Farmers' Program, which trains young people in more efficient methods so they can farm their land in ways that will make the most of its possibilities.

The use of modern farm equipment and methods is increasing as a result of the attention being given to the improvement of Portuguese agriculture. Farm workers now contribute eight percent to the gross national product. This is a great increase over their contribution of only ten years ago.

Industries

Portugal has a long way to go before it is a really modern, industrialized country. At present its productivity lies between twenty-five and thirty

The Complexo das Amoreiras, built in 1986 in Lisbon, is a massive complex of apartments, restaurants, movie theaters, and shops. It is ultramodern in design, all chrome and glass on the outside, and part of Portugal's increasingly twentieth-century look.

percent of the average productivity of other EC countries. One of the main reasons for this lag lies in the slow technological development of Portuguese industry. This hindrance to its progress is being rapidly improved with the help of foreign investment.

There are large, up-to-date shipbuilding and repair yards at Lisbon and Setúbal, with oil terminals under development. Sines on the Alentejo coast, which was once a small fishing town, is being converted into a big port with an oil refinery. It is becoming both badly polluted and very unsightly in the process.

Textiles, clothing, and footwear are Portugal's most important exports. Machinery, foodstuffs (especially tomato concentrates, canned fish, and wine), chemicals, fertilizers, wood, glassware,

A hotel development in the Algarve, near Carvoeiro, hanging like a concrete-and-glass curtain down the cliff. Many stretches of the Algarve coast have been spoiled by the building of such vast hotels, which provide rooms for the increasing number of visitors but ruin the natural scenery the visitors come to enjoy.

pottery, and items made from cork are all valuable products.

Tourism

Tourism is a very important industry in Portugal, with as many as 16 million tourists visiting in a year, just over 12 million of them coming from Spain. These tourists are attracted by the mild climate, the long beaches of fine white sand, and the prices, which once were almost the lowest in Europe but are now rapidly rising. A high proportion of the visitors go to the Algarve, which has 20 percent of the total hotel capacity of the country, second highest after the Lisbon area, which has 26 percent.

Tourism represents a major source of income in foreign currency for Portugal. This is not only brought in by the visitors themselves; a large amount of foreign investment is also attracted to Portugal in the financing of property development, the building of hotels, tourist villages, and apartment buildings.

8

Transportation and Communications

Portugal's road and rail systems run mainly north and south, with only occasional branches eastward into Spain. River traffic, except on the Tagus, is of minor importance, as the rivers are mostly too shallow. The Douro River used to be navigable before being blocked by dams for hydroelectricity.

Trains

Portugal's excellent railroad system is run by a partly state-owned company, the *Companhia dos Caminhos de Ferro Portugueses*. The system is an old one, spreading outward from a few main centers. Some of the lines to remoter areas are still narrow gauge. There are some other old-fashioned survivals in the operation. For example, you can still see women with red flags at local stops signaling for the train to start. The major routes are electrified, while branch lines have diesel engines.

Steam Trains
Two period steam trains still run in Portugal. The Historical Train is pulled by a 1905 German engine and has a mixture of German, Portuguese, and Belgian cars, with a French luggage car. The other is pulled by an 1875 British narrow-gauge engine, with Portuguese, French, and Swiss cars.

There are two kinds of trains: *Directo*, a local train that stops frequently, and *Rápido*, an express as it name suggests, connecting the main towns by a fast route.

The railroad is a comparatively cheap way of getting around Portugal, often cheaper than going by bus. Higher fares are charged on the fast routes, such as the Lisbon/Oporto line. These routes have the most comfortable, modern trains, while the cars that run on the other lines are mostly old and rather uncomfortable to ride in.

The railroad system covers most of the country, reaching to even the smallest mountain town in the north and passing through some of Portugal's most attractive scenery. The Tagus River splits the rail system in half at Lisbon. There is no rail bridge over the river, and to catch a train to the Algarve travelers must take a ferry from the center of the city across to the other bank.

Roads

There are modern superhighways (*auto-estradas*) between Oporto, Lisbon, and Faro. Apart from these few expressways the best roads are the national highways (*estradas nacionais*), but these get very crowded.

While 60 percent of Portugal's roads are paved, it is necessary to drive very slowly on many of the country's roads. Many secondary roads need resurfacing. They tend to have numerous potholes, stray pedestrians, and wandering animals. Donkeys carrying huge loads and flocks of sheep or goats are hazards. The minor roads climb around mountainsides on steep hairpin bends, giving magnificent views to the

A typical scene on a remote country road near a small village in the Alentejo. You can never tell exactly what lies around the next bend!

passengers but making the driver's job even more difficult. Still, the road network has improved enormously. Only 30 years ago 13 percent of the population lived in villages that could not be reached by road. In rural areas some Portuguese still travel by horse or oxcart.

The Portuguese are notoriously careless drivers, with one of the highest accident rates in Europe. The speed limit is 74 mph (120 kph) on the superhighways. On other open roads the limit is 56 mph (90 kph), and 31 to 37 mph (50 to 60 kph) in built-up areas, depending on traffic density.

Air transportation

For a small country, Portugal is well served by planes. The national airline is TAP/Air Portugal (*Transportes Aéreos Portugueses*), which also flies regularly between the mainland, Madeira, and the Azores, as well as on international routes. It has an internal subsidiary, LAR, which serves smaller towns.

The three main airports are Lisbon, Oporto, and Faro, all with international flights. Faro, in the Algarve, has built a new airport terminal to take care of the huge number of vacationers who flood in from other parts of Europe. The distances within Portugal are so small that only a few business people really need to get around by air. There are also international airports at Santa Maria in the Azores and Funchal, Madeira.

Television and radio

There are just two television channels in Portugal, both broadcasting in color, and both of

---

Newspapers

Portugal is well supplied with newspapers, including about 30 daily papers in all. There are five morning and three evening papers published every day in Lisbon, three morning papers in Oporto, and six main national weekly papers. They cover the whole range of political opinion from left to right. The *Diário Noticias*, a Lisbon daily, is the most important and probably the most independently written newspaper, even though it is state-owned. There is also a daily newspaper devoted entirely to sports.

---

them state-controlled. In comparison with American television, neither of them is very adventurous. As Portuguese is also spoken in Brazil, which has a population 13 times larger than Portugal, Brazilian soap operas are imported to boost the local programming. Programs with English soundtracks are usually screened with Portuguese subtitles.

As television reception can be difficult in many of the mountainous areas of the country, radio still plays an important part in Portuguese life. There are four radio stations that broadcast nationwide, three of them state-controlled. New regulations passed in 1988 have allowed many local radio stations catering to regional interests to open up.

People are required to have licenses for their radios. Fees for licenses are included in their utility bills.

9

The People and Their Way of Life

The people of Portugal still show the ethnic characteristics of those who lived in the country in its early days. They tend to be dark-haired, of medium height, and sturdily built, much like the Celtic Lusitanians who were among the first known settlers. In the north of the country, there are also taller, fair-looking people, whose

A woman dressed in traditional black doing the day's shopping. This is a cobbled street in a fishing village on the Atlantic coast, but it could be in any Portuguese town, with the laundry hung to dry outside typical whitewashed houses.

65

forebears may have been Germanic. In the south, there are many who resemble the Arabic Moors who lived there for five centuries.

The Portuguese personality is very different from that of their Spanish neighbors. In contrast to the Spaniards' noisy exuberance, the Portuguese are quieter and more dignified, almost old-fashioned. Older Portuguese dress in a reserved way. In the country districts many older women still dress in traditional mourning black. Younger people, however, are very trendy, with a great sense of fashion. They wear the latest styles, many of them copied from international originals but made in Portugal.

The Portuguese have a very strong sense of the importance of the family. Though several million of them (known as "guest workers") have emigrated, or work in restaurants and factories throughout Europe, they send money home regularly. This steady inflow of foreign currency has been a vital help to the Portuguese economy, although it is a little less important since the EC investments started to flow in.

A clear example of family solidarity was shown after Portugal lost her African colonies in 1974-75. Many of the 750,000 refugees who returned to their homeland were welcomed by their relatives, who helped them to find work or start a business, and generally adjust to their new lives.

Because the family ties are so close, there are always grandmothers or aunts to look after children while the parents go to work. Those members of a family who live in the city usually have close relatives in several parts of Portugal to go and stay with during their vacations.

Where the Portuguese live

In the main cities, Portuguese families live in apartments. These are in old buildings if they are in the center of town or in modern highrises in the newly built areas on the outskirts. In Lisbon, the apartment buildings are painted in many colors, giving the city a brightly patterned look.

In the smaller towns and the rural areas, the Portuguese live in houses, mostly built of stone, whose design used to vary tremendously from one part of the country to another. Now that rural areas are no longer so cut off from each other, the days of traditional regional design have almost gone, and the houses are built in a similarly modern style all over the country.

In the colder northern inland areas, the houses are usually warmed by open fires and have big

A contrast between the old and the new. A row of rundown old houses in front of a new white apartment building. One of the old houses has its front tiled with a modern version of traditional blue-and-white tiles and is topped by a cluster of TV aerials. The house next door, with a pointed roof, was whitewashed a long time ago.

chimneys. In the south, the houses are whitewashed to reflect the summer heat and have colorfully painted woodwork for doors and window frames.

Language

The national language of Portugal is Portuguese. It is also the language of Brazil, once a Portuguese colony, so it is spoken in one form or another by around 130 million people worldwide. It is one of the family of Romance (or Latin) languages that includes French, Italian, Spanish, and Rumanian. The Latin spoken in Portugal for the 600 years of the Roman occupation formed a solid basis for today's Portuguese.

The Portuguese language looks like Spanish on the printed page but is pronounced very differently. Spoken Portuguese has a softer sound than Spanish does, with the words run

---

Unusual Sounds

Among the peculiarities of Portuguese is the "ng" sound that is made in the nose. Another is shown by the *tilde* sign (˜) on the letter *a* or *o*. São (saint) sounds something like sa-ow-ng, all run together, with the last two sounds sung in the nose. A similar nasal sound is made on words ending with *n* or *m*. They are pronounced as if there were a *g* there, too: *bon* becomes bong, *jardim* (garden) becomes jardeeng.

The letter *s* is pronounced "sh" before hard consonants and at the end of words: the town Cascais sounds like Cashkaish. There is a constant soft "sh" sound when a Portuguese is speaking.

---

together more often. It is quite difficult for an English-speaker to understand at first, since many parts of a sentence just disappear when pronounced.

Many Portuguese learn to speak at least one language other than their own. This second language may be English, French, or the Spanish of their close neighbor.

An elegant eighteenth-century house standing on the banks of the Gilão River in Tavira, Algarve. This typical kind of well-proportioned house can be found all over the country. Details may change from area to area, but the carved stone around the windows, the whitewashed walls, the tiled roof, and the careful spacing of the windows and door are the same everywhere.

Religion

Ninety-four and a half percent of Portuguese are Roman Catholic. The depth and age-old nature of their faith can best be seen in the popularity of *romarias* (religious festivals), which are held all over the country and date back many centuries. Every town and village has its own saint's day that it celebrates with a festival, so hardly a day

Fátima
The most famous place of pilgrimage in Portugal is not a very old one. In 1917, during World War I, the Virgin Mary is reputed to have appeared six times to three shepherd children at Fátima and asked them to pray for the peace of the world. Now there is a huge church on the spot where the vision was seen, visited by hundreds of thousands of pilgrims every year. One of the children, Lúcia, now a very old lady, is still alive and a nun. She attended the fiftieth anniversary celebrations of the first vision. There were 1.5 million pilgrims at the ceremony conducted by Pope Paul VI.

passes without a local holiday somewhere in Portugal. These traditional Catholic celebrations are usually very colorful affairs, with processions in traditional costume, bagpipers, fireworks, and people crowding into town from the surrounding countryside. A romaria is often celebrated with a country fair.

One of the most attractive festivals is the ancient Festa dos Tabuleiros, held in Tomar on the first Sunday in July on alternate years. It is a kind of harvest festival. Around 400 young girls, who are dressed in white, take part in a procession. They wear tall, elaborate headdresses made out of loaves of bread in a wicker framework decorated with brightly colored paper flowers and wheat. They are usually accompanied by their boyfriends, who walk with them to make sure that the weight on their heads doesn't topple them over. After the procession the bread is distributed to the poor of the town.

Education

Portuguese education is modeled on the French system of education. Most schools are state operated, although there are some private schools that are also now recognized by the government. These are run by Roman Catholic organizations, such as the Dominicans or Jesuits.

Many Portuguese children start their education in a nursery school (*infantil* or *pre primario*), which they can attend from four to six years old. These schools are not yet available all over the country. Compulsory education starts at the age of six, when children go into grade one in primary school (*primario* or *basico*). They stay there until they are 12, going through grades one to five.

At 12 children move on to secondary school (*escola secundária*) where they start in the sixth grade and reach the ninth when they are 15. At that time they have the chance to do two more years in the tenth and eleventh grades, to gain the standard of education that will equip them for a better job later or get them into a university. Since the late 1960s, more and more teenagers have taken this option.

The curriculum is the equivalent of that taught in most European schools. The subjects are science, math, physics, geography, history, and, of course, Portuguese language and literature. French and English are taught as the two main compulsory foreign languages. Spanish is not usually on the curriculum. It is so similar to

Portuguese that it is easy for students to pick it up as they go along. In some schools German is offered in tenth and eleventh grades.

Beginning at age six, children are tested regularly and have to take annual exams. Exams are marked from 0 to 20, with 10 as the passing grade. If students fail the annual exam they have to repeat the year. The rate of failure in some of the more deprived parts of the country currently exceeds 40 percent for those taking the main exam at the age of 15. This high failure rate reflects the

Recess at a village school in the valley of the Douro River. This kind of local school has suffered from a serious lack of financing in recent years but still provides a basic education for the children of its immediate region.

In School

Portugal is seriously short of school space. In Lisbon, Oporto, and other main towns, there is such a demand for classrooms that classes have to be held in shifts, with some even being held in the evening. Ideally, hours run from 8:30 or 9:00 a.m. to 3:00 or 3:30 p.m., Monday to Friday, with classes also on Saturday morning. Classes last for 50 minutes.

It is very rare for a school to provide school meals, and pupils have to eat any lunch they have brought with them in the normal break between classes.

poor general standard of education in the population at large. Only 84 percent of Portuguese over the age of 15 can read. In comparison, the literacy rate in France is 99 percent; in Greece it is 95 percent.

There are three semesters a year: from the beginning of October to December 18, followed by two weeks of vacation at Christmas. The second runs from early January to Easter, when there are another two weeks' vacation. The school year finishes in mid-June. This means that the summer vacation runs all the way from mid-June to early October. There are no vacations during the terms.

Investment from the EC is being used to try to upgrade Portugal's educational situation as fast as possible, with huge sums of money being invested in building and equipping schools and training teachers. Only major city schools have computers. Pupils also have to provide all school materials, including books. Because there is no room to store them in school overnight, pupils have to carry all their books, workbooks, and papers to and from home every day.

Higher education

Formerly there were only three universities in Portugal: Coimbra, the oldest, Lisbon, and Oporto. Because of the country's overwhelming poverty and the impossibility of getting around easily, this meant that only the rich or those living near those cities could acquire higher education. More universities have been founded since the mid 1970s, and there are now eight, scattered all over the country. There are also schools devoted to different types of education, such as vocational and business skills, as well as teachers' training colleges in all the provincial centers.

Health

Portuguese doctors are among the best in Europe, although they still do not have the support of ultramodern equipment with which to work. The latest technology, using scanners, dialysis machines, and transplant surgery, which is fairly common in the United States, costs a great deal of money. Portugal has only recently been able to begin equipping its hospitals with such advanced resources. There is one doctor to about every 400 persons. This is very close to the number of doctors to persons in our country. The Portuguese medical community makes up for a certain lack of expensive equipment by being well-trained and caring.

Portugal has a National Health Service (*Serviço Medico Sociais*) similar to Britain's or Canada's.

A saint's day celebration in a village near Alcobaça. On such occasions as well as on national holidays villagers may be joined by relatives and other vacationers.

Unfortunately, like other national health services it is a huge bureaucracy, and waiting for surgery, unless it is an emergency, can take a long time. Whenever they can afford to, the Portuguese go to a private doctor and pay out-of-pocket for their medical care. For this reason there tend to be more doctors available in the big cities and in the richer areas like the Algarve than in the poorer districts. When they are ill, the Portuguese often consult the local pharmacist.

Vacations
Most Portuguese do not take formal vacations with tour groups. With the family network spread all over the country, it is always possible to visit

How the Portuguese Spend Their Money
The average Portuguese family spends up to
40 percent of its income on rent. The highest
rents are in the cities. The remaining 60
percent is spent as follows:

Food and drink	48.6%
Clothing and shoes	10.7%
Housing costs (not rent)	13.3%
Health	2.8%
Transportation and communications	14.6%
Education and entertainment	4.3%
Tobacco	1.3%
Miscellaneous	4.4%

aunts by the sea or uncles in the mountains during those long summer school vacations.

There are 13 national holiday days a year, when everything closes. Liberation Day, which celebrates the revolution, is on April 25 and is the most important national holiday. Added to these, the local saints' days all over the country greatly increase the number of possible holidays to be enjoyed by the Portuguese.

10   Food and Drink

Portuguese food tends to be simple and traditionally cooked. Refrigerators and freezers are not widely owned as in the United States, although they are much more common in the cities than in the country. As a result the Portuguese shop daily for fresh food, eating whatever is best that day in the markets.

The fruit, vegetable, and flower market in Funchal, Madeira. Farmers from all around the island bring their produce to sell at this colorful central market.

Soup

Soup (*sopa*) appears at most main meals and is often a hearty dish that is almost a meal in itself. Two very popular soups are: *açorda* from the Alentejo, which has a basis of bread soaked in olive oil, herbs, and sometimes eggs or fish; and *caldo verde*, from the Minho, made with cabbage, clear broth, and slices of peppery sausage.

Meat

Pork is Portugal's principal meat and can appear in all sorts of dishes. One of the most unusual is *porco com amêijoas* (pork with clams), a kind of stew, with tiny clams still in their shells. Beef can be expensive and tough and is consequently not very popular, although veal is. One unusual meat is kid, young goat, which is eaten roasted in the same way as lamb. It is especially tasty in those parts of the country where kids graze on wild herbs.

Fish

Fish is cheaper than meat and is a favorite food. Portuguese fishing boats trawl the Atlantic, which is still comparatively clean. Fish caught there are safer to eat than fish from the seriously

Bacalhau

A staple ingredient of Portuguese cooking is dried, salted cod (*bacalhau*), which can be seen hanging from hooks in grocery stores in large, hard, flat chunks. It has to be soaked in several changes of water for 24 hours before cooking.

The main fish market on the island of Madeira. The fishmongers are cutting tunafish into thick steaks. Fishing in the unpolluted ocean around Madeira produces large catches. Besides tuna, local fishermen land swordfish, red mullet, and conger eels.

polluted Mediterranean. The traditional fishing boat has a high prow, supposedly of Phoenician origin, with a symbol, such as an eye, painted on it to protect it from evil.

A great variety of fish is caught, with swordfish and tuna among the largest. The catch is sold at dockside fish markets as soon as the boats return, or on the open beach where the boats are drawn up. Since nowhere is farther than 140 miles from the coast, the fish arrive still very fresh even in the markets near the Spanish border.

Desserts
The Portuguese love rich desserts. Their sweets are mostly made with sugar and eggs and often have amusing names like "bacon from heaven"

(*toucinho de ceú*) or "angels' chests" (*papos de anjo*). One of the most popular desserts is *arroz doce*, a cold rice pudding made with eggs, sugar, and cinnamon.

In the Algarve all kinds of fancy shapes, such as birds, animals, and baskets of flowers are made out of almond paste, a legacy from the days of the Moors.

Wine

Grapes have been grown in Portugal at least since the time of the Romans. As in the rest of southern Europe, wine in Portugal is an everyday drink and is very reasonably priced. Portugal is the sixth largest world producer of wine, with around 220 million gallons (10 million hectoliters) a year. Most of the wine is made in central and northern Portugal, and every small area produces its own local type.

A wine that is unique to Portugal is *vinho verde*, "green wine." It is so called because it is wine that is drunk when it is newly made, not because it is green colored. It can be either straw-gold or red, and both are drunk cold. Vinho verde mostly comes from vineyards east and north of Oporto. The grapes are picked before they are completely ripe. The resulting wine continues to ferment in the bottle and is slightly bubbly.

The wine for which Portugal is most famous is port, whose name comes from the city of Oporto. The grapes from which port is made are grown in the special soil of hillside terraces along the Upper Douro valley. The soil comes from schist, a yellowish rock that splits and can retain moisture. Wine production here has been protected by law

A grape picker, in a vineyard in the Serra da Estrela, carrying the grapes she has picked in a box on her head. Portugal has a wide variety of types of wine, often produced in small quantities from the grapes of local vineyards, such as this one, to be drunk by the families that own the vines.

since 1757. The grapes were once trodden in great vats, by men working in four-hour shifts, their legs stained red with the juice. Today, the crushing is mostly done by machinery.

The wine used to be shipped down the Douro, but now that the river is dammed, it is carried in tanker trucks the 100 miles (160 kilometers) to Oporto, where it is stored in "lodges" (warehouses). Port is blended from three parts partly fermented wine and one part brandy. Vintage port, heavy and sweet, has to mature in wooden casks for over 20 years.

Many of the oldest Oporto firms dealing in port were founded by British merchants in the eighteenth century and still have British names like Sandeman, Croft, and Taylor.

Madeira

The island of Madeira, which is mountainous and has a very pleasant climate, is famous for its sweet wine, which is called Madeira.

The soil of the island of Madeira is especially suitable for growing grapevines. It is a mixture of volcanic ash and clay and light red in color. The vines are grown on terraces carved out of the mountainsides. Vegetables grow in among the vines, making the most of both scarce water and good soil, and benefiting from the shade of the vines.

The best Madeira wine is aged in oak casks in heated rooms for a long time, as much as 25 years or more. One of the odd characteristics of Madeira is that its flavor is actually improved by being shaken around as in a sailing ship traveling through the heat of the tropics on the way to the West Indies. Barrels of wine used to be shipped there and back, simply to produce a better wine.

Like many other wines, Madeira also improves by being aged in the bottle. It is possible to drink wine that was bottled 150 years ago. The famous English statesman Winston Churchill used to visit the island and paint pictures there. He was once enjoying a glass of Madeira and remarked on the fact that it had been made at the time of the French Revolution.

11 Sports and the Arts and Crafts

As in many other European countries, soccer is by far the most popular sport in Portugal. There are three major teams that play in European Cup games: Sporting and Benfica, both from Lisbon, and Oporto. Benfica was the team that the world-famous Eusébio played for.

Hockey on roller skates also has a large following. Swimming at the less dangerous beaches, particularly along the south coast, is a favorite way of cooling off in summer. Inland there are good municipal pools in many towns, as well as stretches of river excellent for swimming.

There are some world-class golf courses, especially in the Algarve, but this is more a sport for visiting tourists than for the Portuguese themselves.

Bullfighting

Portuguese bullfighting (*tourada*) is much less popular than it once was. Soccer overtook it in popularity long ago. The same is true of bullfighting in Spain. Bullfighting in Portugal, however, is very different from the Spanish version. For one thing, the fighting is done on horseback, with the rider (*cavaleiro*) dressed in full eighteenth-century costume of a gold-embroidered coat, three-cornered hat, and thigh boots with silver spurs. The highly bred horse is well trained in the kind of prancing step for which the lovely white Lipizzaner horses of the Spanish

Riding School of Vienna are famous. The result is a kind of skillful dance between the horse and the bull. The other important difference is that the bull is not killed in the Portuguese ring.

Portuguese arts

Portuguese music, literature, and painting are almost unknown outside Portugal. It is, for instance, difficult to find translations of Portuguese books into English.

During the years when Salazar was dictator, artistic expression was smothered by censorship. Since the revolution there has been almost complete freedom for artists and writers to do as they please. Nowadays, the arts are heavily sponsored by money from the Gulbenkian Foundation. Calouste Gulbenkian was an Armenian millionaire who made his money from oil. When he died in 1955, he left his magnificent art collection and his fortune, now worth over a billion dollars, to Portugal, where he had spent his last years. The foundation supports education and the arts with scholarships, libraries, museums, and the funding of orchestras, ballet companies, and choirs.

Music

The truly national music of Portugal is *fado*, a form of folk singing that is melancholy and sentimental. It is thought to have begun with the songs of the medieval troubadors and probably gets its name from the Latin word for destiny, *fatum*. It is essentially music of the cities and seems to be most at home in the poorer parts of Lisbon, like the Alfama. Lisbon and Coimbra

A fado singer performing at one of Lisbon's most famous fado restaurants, mainly for the enjoyment of tourists. Other nightspots feature less sophisticated versions of this kind of folksinging both in Lisbon and the university town of Coimbra.

each has its own style of fado singing. Lisbon's is the more gutsy of the two, sung by a single singer, more often a woman than a man, accompanied by two guitars. The Coimbra version, which is mostly sung by the university students, is more sentimental and romantic.

Literature

An epic poem, *Os Lusíados (The Lusiads)*, published in 1572, is the most famous of all early Portuguese writing. It is the story of Vasco da Gama's voyage to India, written by Luis de Camoẽs (1524 to 1580), who had followed da Gama's route himself. He was shipwrecked on the way and could describe his hero's adventures from personal experience.

In the eighteenth century and after, there was considerable French influence on Portuguese literature. Manuel M.B. du Bocage, born in 1765, was a wild character of French descent and was often in serious trouble with the authorities. He joined the army and later the marines, traveling to Brazil, India, and Africa. His lyric and satirical poems are some of the best ever written in Portuguese.

In the nineteenth century, novelists began to deal with social problems. One of the few to gain an international reputation was Eça de Queiroz (born in 1845), who attacked certain deficiencies of the clergy and the inadequacy of middle-class education, as well as other social ills. Disillusioned with life in Portugal, he went to live in Paris, where he died in 1900.

Fernando Pessoa (1888-1935) was a poet who wrote his verse under three *noms de plume*, (writer's names), each one reflecting a totally different side of his nature.

Architecture

Although there is very little building left from the time of the Moors, the style of houses in the south was strongly influenced by their architectural styles. Typical Algarve houses are whitewashed and cube-shaped, with elaborately pierced chimney pots, like lanterns.

The great buildings from Portugal's past are the monasteries and churches that survive from the days after the Reconquest. They were massively solid, built almost as severely as the castles.

In the eighteenth century, elaborately gilded and painted church interiors were created, often

A carved arcade at the Palace Hotel, Buçaco. Once a royal hunting lodge, the building has elaborate carvings in the Manueline style. The Portuguese stonemasons have been developing their skills since the 1500s.

Manueline Architecture

The vast riches that poured into Portugal in the early 1500s were used for lavish building projects. The fanciful style of decoration that was employed became known as Manueline, after King Manuel I. This decoration was partly inspired by the art of the Moors, with its geometric designs, and partly it was just fantasy. The huge window in the monastery at Tomar (shown on page 19) is a good example.

Queluz Palace, on the outskirts of Lisbon, was built 1758-94 as a summer palace. It became a permanent one when the main palace burned down. It was modeled on the French palace of Versailles, although it is tiny in comparison. The name is taken from the Arabic Qu'al-Luz, ''the valley of the almond tree.''

by redecorating older, less ornate churches. Elegant houses, designed in a formal way, with evenly spaced windows, pillars, and statues were also popular then. Some of the best examples of this kind of architecture can be seen in the handsome streets and squares that the Portuguese politician Pombal built in Lisbon to replace those destroyed in the 1755 earthquake.

The picture of one elegant country house of the time, the Solar de Mateus (1743), appears on the label of the Mateus wine bottles. Another fine example is just outside Lisbon, at Queluz, where a royal palace built in 1758 was modeled on Versailles in France, though it is much smaller. However, it does have elaborate gardens like the original.

Azulejos - Portuguese Tiles

The walls of churches, houses, railroad stations, and buildings of every kind all over Portugal are decorated with pictures made of tiles called *azulejos*. It is Portugal's most popular art form. These *tapetes* (tile tapestries) began to be used in the mid 1500s, the idea coming from Spain, where they were created by the Moors. The most popular color for them has always been shades of blue, which is where the name comes from. *Azul* means "blue." Azulejos have many advantages. They last almost forever without their colors fading; they are easy to clean; and they keep rooms cool in the summer. They are used indoors and out. Sometimes they cover the entire front of a building.

A detail of wall tiles (azulejos) in Viseu, Beira Alta. These particular tiles show country scenes, but religious stories or pictures of famous battles were also very popular. Azulejos, which are used both inside and outside houses and churches, make very practical wall coverings.

89

In the nineteenth century, there was a fashion for copying styles of the past. Buildings were a blend of Moorish, Gothic, and other old fashions. One of the most fanciful is the Castelo da Pena, built in the 1840s as an extension to a genuine medieval convent, on a hilltop high above the town of Sintra. A figure of Triton, with tree roots growing from his head and his legs ending in fish tails, holds up a balcony. The roof of the palace is embellished with Arab minarets, Gothic turrets, and a big dome.

Much of the most striking architecture from the end of the nineteenth century was also in imitation of earlier styles, especially of Manueline. One of the main railroad stations in Lisbon, Rossio Station, a very fancy affair with lots of carving and tiled walls, was designed in imitation Manueline (1891). So was the magnificent royal hunting lodge at Buçaco. It was created by the scene painter of the royal opera and finished in 1907. It stands in an ancient forest of trees imported from many countries.

The best modern building in Portugal has been more functional than decorative. It is the April 25 Bridge across the Tagus. Originally called the Salazar Bridge, it was renamed in honor of the revolution. This bridge is a soaring suspension design with the longest central span in Europe. Oporto has three fine bridges, one of them a double-decker, crossing the Douro. The museum of the Gulbenkian Foundation in Lisbon is as attractive for its modern design and beautiful gardens as it is for its collection of works of art. One of the most striking modern buildings in Portugal is the Amoreiras Complex on the

The craft of tiling is very ancient. Here a tiler is reroofing a house with the traditional tiles that have been used since Roman times. These tiles are made locally along with other clay products.

outskirts of Lisbon. This collection of huge square reflecting towers was designed by Tomás Taveira and looks rather like a vast modern version of an ancient castle.

Crafts

Portugal is still a country where handicrafts are practiced everywhere, just as they have been for hundreds of years. However, this is a way of life under serious threat as the Portuguese are trying to develop their economy. It is much easier and cheaper to mold things from plastic than to craft them laboriously by hand.

Apart from the production of azulejos, there are many other kinds of attractive ceramics to be

91

seen all over Portugal. Each region and even specific towns have developed their own styles. Barcelos makes colorful roosters, which are the symbol of the town, and also all sorts of imaginary figurines: humorous devils, birds playing instruments, or animals singing. Coimbra and Alcobaça make attractive blue-and-white pottery, not unlike the china in the same colors that comes from Delft in Holland. Caldas da Rainha is famous for green-glazed plates made to look like big leaves. Vila Real specializes in black-glazed ware. In the Alentejo, potters are still making big terracotta jars of the same shape as those that were made by the Romans.

Lacemaking
The island of Madeira has been famous for fine lace tablecloths, shawls, and embroidered handkerchiefs and blouses for over 100 years. The craft was sponsored by an Englishwoman, a Mrs. Phelps. In the nineteenth century, she opened an embroidery school for women whose families had been impoverished by a blight that had ruined the grape harvest. Unfortunately, this craft is very time-consuming, and today fewer people are practicing this handiwork.

Cork and leather
Another Portuguese craft is making articles from cork. The best cork oak forests are in the Alentejo. Cork is used in bulletin boards, floor and wall coverings, and bottle stoppers among other things. It is a particularly good insulating material, so Portugal is famous for its buckets with lids (*tarros*) that are used to keep food hot or

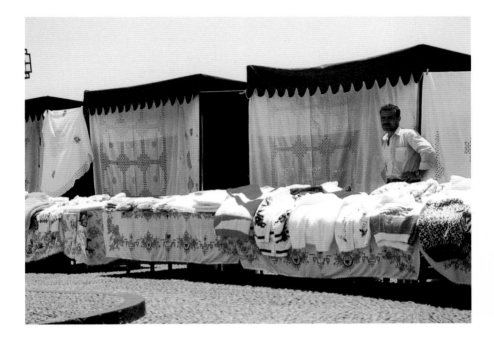

Lacemaking is an important craft in Madeira. This vendor has a range of lace ware for sale as well as locally made knitwear — another local craft.

cold. The *tarros* also make excellent ice buckets.

Although it is more of an industry than a craft these days, shoes and boots are made all over the country. In the cities, shoe stores sell the latest fashion in shoes. However, there are still many country bootmakers at work, and there is rarely a local market day without a stand where you can buy strong leather boots.

Weaving

The Arraiolos people in the Alentejo have been making embroidered rugs in lovely colors and bold designs for centuries. Many of the exquisite patterns go back to Moorish designs, but they have been changed very freely through the centuries and now have a character all of their own. These embroidered rugs sell for a great deal of money in the tourist shops.

Portalegre in the Alto Alentejo has had a woolen industry for centuries. There is a factory there that produces tapestries, which are woven pictures, often copies of paintings. The tight weave consists of 210,000 knots per square yard (250,000 knots per square meter), so it is not surprising that a tapestry might take several years to make.

*   *   *

A sleeping beauty awakes
After nearly fifty years under an oppressive dictatorship, Portugal was one of the poorest and least developed countries in Europe. However, since it joined the European Community in 1986, millions of dollars have been flooding into Portugal from richer countries. This new wealth is being spent by Portugal in an intense effort to catch up with the more advanced countries.

The recent changes as a result of this effort have been spectacular. Portugal has always been a very beautiful country, from its wide plains to its richly forested mountains. Now it is fast becoming an up-to-date nation as well.

Index

© Heinemann Children's Reference 1991
This edition originally published 1991 by
Heinemann Children's Reference, a division
of Heinemann Educational Books, Ltd.